Ideas About Creating Ideas

Tips, tricks & principles to help
you create great work every day.

Other titles for this book
also considered by the author:

The Secrets of Making Great Work

How To Get Ahead in the Creative Industry

A Creative Director's Notebook

Mini Pep Talks for Creatives

*Creative Principles To
Help You Make Better Work*

*Do What Makes You Giggle:
A creative guide to staying happy
and producing your best work*

IDEAS ABOUT CREATING IDEAS

Tips, tricks & principles to help you create great work every day.

Martin Homent

Ideas About Creating Ideas
*Tips, tricks & principles to help
you create great work every day.*

Copyright © Martin Homent 2024

ISBN: 978-1-7385199-0-3

First published in February 2024.

Written, designed and set by Martin Homent.
www.martinhoment.com

All rights reserved. No part of this publication may be reproduced, distributed, or
transmitted in any form or by any means, including photocopying, recording, or any
other electronic or mechanical methods, without the prior written permission of
the author, except in the case of brief quotations embodied in critical reviews and
certain other non-commercial uses permitted by copyright law.

For Emma and Cinnamon,

A constant source of joy and inspiration.

You probably gave me the idea to write this book.

Or maybe it was you, Emma.

Contents

Introduction 11
Author's note 13

No question is too stupid 15
Don't present anything you don't want
your client to choose........................... 17
Know your most creative time of day 19
Keep a bottom drawer of your
best unsold ideas 21
Don't knock other work 23
Time off is as important as time on 25
Start with writing.............................. 27
Do more of what makes you giggle............... 29
Create first, edit later......................... 31
Write down ideas when they happen............. 33
Be kind to yourself............................ 35
Keep it simple 37
Input is as important as output 39
Don't ever think you're the finished article 41
Work with those who do what you can't........... 43
Done is better than perfect..................... 45
Awards aren't everything...................... 47
Use your creativity beyond your day job 49
Nobody can sell your work like you can 51
Everybody's making it up as they go along........ 53
Know your superpower......................... 55
Never stop learning 57
Explain the idea in one sentence 59
Find your people.............................. 61
Master the art, not the software 63
Borrow and steal, but never copy 65

Don't let the word 'no' get to you	67
Learn everything you can about the subject in your brief	69
The closer you are to clients, the closer you are to success	71
Build your happy place	73
Late isn't always great.	75
Know when to stop.	77
What worked this time won't always work next time	79
Look after your mind: it's your greatest asset	81
See every problem as a creative opportunity	83
Be your own Hype Man	85
Leave room for happy accidents	87
If you have the idea, you can make it happen.	89
Quality follows quantity	91
The perfect brief doesn't exist	93
Don't wait for your ideas to happen.	95
Bring people on your journey	97
Use the overnight test	99
Trust your gut	101
Selling the idea is as important as having the idea	103
Even creative directors need a creative director	105
You are not defined by your job title	107
The most inspiring thing isn't always on the brief	109
There is always another way	111
Don't judge yourself by others' success	113

F*ck likes, do what you love 115
Make every element of your execution
express your idea............................... 117
Saying 'no' is no bad thing........................ 119
A connected creative hobby can
unlock your mind 121
Don't panic! 123
Review rough thoughts,
present finished ideas...........................125
Make improvements, not changes 127
Present however many ideas are
right for your problem...........................129
Some work feeds your bank account,
other work feeds your soul 131
Network beyond where you work.................133
Beware of the brainstorm!......................135
Failure is your best teacher..................... 137
Pick your battles................................139
Small brands can provide your
biggest opportunities 141
Be the spark....................................143
To think outside the box,
make sure there's a box 145
Leadership is a mindset, not a job title............ 147
The third idea you present should push
the furthest 149
Big ideas don't always need big budgets 151
Know your worth 153
No day is wasted................................155
Energy and hard work beats talent 157
Make a note of what works 159

Acknowledgements............................ *161*
About the author *163*

Introduction

If you could travel back in time 25 years and give yourself all the wisdom you'd accumulated during that period, what would you say?

This was the spark that ignited the idea for this book and a question I was asked when I was a guest on a podcast to talk about my career as a creative in the advertising industry.

Wanting to make sure I had a suitable answer, I began writing down all the things I had learnt. In a few hours, I went from 'I'm not sure' to 'here's ten things'. The more I wrote, the more I remembered.

I also dug out some of my old notebooks where, if there was a problem I had or something not quite right in the agency I worked at, I'd write down ideas of how I'd overcome the issue (a useful habit I still have). In a few days I had over 50 insights.

This was feeling less like an answer to a question and more like a book. Sometimes ideas have a way of telling you what they need to be, so I decided to listen and write this book.

You may be a student looking to get into the industry or perhaps you're also a creative director, agency leader or responsible for inspiring a team of people. Whatever stage you're at, I think there's something in this book that can help you.

A lot has changed in the last 25 years: technology has sped things up and we demand ideas quicker; clients use data and algorithms to make safer choices, wanting to ensure ideas work before they buy them;

and agencies have become more like corporate businesses by adopting open-plan working and combining smaller agencies into larger places of work. All of these changes mean we need to keep hold of and remind ourselves of what it takes to make great work.

Principles, pep talks, cheat codes — call them what you will, but in this book are 73 useful things I picked up along the way that have made a difference not just to my work, but also how I work. So much so, I still rely on them today. They have helped me create award-winning campaigns, become a creative director before I reached 30 and even collaborate with one of my creative heroes, Prince.

There is a tip on every page of the book and it's designed for you to dip in and out of when you need it. Think of it as a creative companion and guide to help navigate the daily challenges of creating work.

Equally, you can read this from beginning to end, like a traditional book. And finally, I have linked each tip to another connected one in the book, so it can work like a choose your own adventure.

Try them. Keep what works. Improve on what doesn't. Let me know how you get on (my contact details are in the back of the book) if you like. The most important thing is that you never stop creating and never let anything get in your way.

Oh, and if your creativity leads to making a time machine, take a copy of this book back for me.

Author's note

This book was written based on my learning and experience of working in the advertising industry — commercial creativity, rather than art (although the advice may be useful for you if you're a creative person specialising in another area).

I have a strong belief that creativity is something in all of us, but some people choose to embrace and nurture it and a lucky few even make a living out of it. Throughout the book I will refer to those people as 'creative people' or a 'creative' (plural 'creatives').

I will also often refer to the company a creative works for as an 'agency', as this is my experience. However, the same is true if you work in-house, for a studio, as part of a user experience team, as a freelance photographer or film-maker, or if you work for any other creative business.

I will also talk a lot about 'the work' or 'work'. By this I mean creative work — the ideas and the things that are produced to express them: films, posters, adverts, experiences, social media posts, user interfaces, digital products... and so on.

NO
?UESTION
is too stupid

Whether we're new to something or have been doing it for years, we can all learn something we don't yet know.

The fear of asking questions can be a barrier to learning. (Or perhaps it's the fear of looking stupid, as you don't know something.) This fear tends to increase if you're in a group.

Google has built its entire business on people searching for something they don't know. It happens millions of times per second. Yet, we tend to feel vulnerable when this happens outside of a search bar, in the comfort and privacy of our own devices.

Whether you're in a room full of people and someone is describing something you don't quite understand or a thought occurs to you during the day and you don't have the answer, ask someone who might.

Many other people in the room will exhale and think: 'Thank God someone asked that question! I didn't know the answer and was too afraid to ask.' The person you ask in any situation will also no doubt delight in passing on their knowledge. After all, they didn't know the answer once either.

A creative mind is a curious mind. Don't leave any question you have unanswered. Ask a question every time you don't know something. You will look interested and engaged, never stupid.

Nobody has all the answers. Turn to *Everybody's making it up as they go along*, on page 53, to find out more.

IDEAS ABOUT CREATING IDEAS

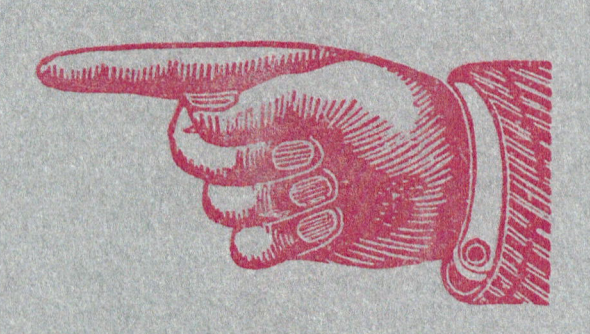

Don't
present
anything
you
don't
want
your
client
to
choose

Unlike a review with a creative director, where it's useful to share a lot of ideas and get their direction on what's working, sharing work with a client is quite the opposite.

Agencies and creative studios often like to show their clients a range of ideas, and usually three is the magic number. If you have two ideas or creative approaches, you may be tempted to include a third that you feel is not as strong as the other two.

You must resist.*

By adding another idea to make up the numbers, you run the risk that this 'lesser option' will be chosen by the client. If it is, you'll be disappointed — secretly hoping they had picked one of the other two.

Regardless of how many ideas you are presenting, you should only show work that you're willing for the client to choose and you'll be happy making. If something doesn't light the fire in your belly, don't share it. Take this approach and you're guaranteed that, whatever your client chooses, you'll be excited by and you'll continue to build a strong body of work.

You can overdo and overthink creative work, see *Know when to stop*, on page 77, for more.

---

*Whatever you do, don't mock up something to show them how awful it is. You're just making the work a reality and therefore easy to buy.

IDEAS ABOUT CREATING IDEAS

Know your

MOST
CREATIVE

time of day

A career in the creative industry means being responsible for producing ideas every day. But that doesn't mean they arrive every minute of every day.

People tend to have moments when there's an internal energy and ideas are bursting to get out.

Some people are at their most creatively productive late at night when everyone else has gone home. The distractions have left the building, the music comes on, the beers come out... and the real creative work begins.

Some will swear by having moments of concentrated focus during the day — popping on a pair of headphones to prevent interruptions and getting their heads down for a 'power hour' of productivity before taking a break.

And others, like myself, wake up full of creative energy. This energy gets used up as the day goes on, tailing off in the afternoon and evening. As I know this is how my mind works, I dedicate the morning to getting down my ideas and try to push any meetings to the afternoon.

It's easy for others to think that, because you're not in a meeting, you're not doing anything, so blocking your diary with thinking time helps protect you from any unwanted distractions.

Whatever you find works for you, if you get to know your most creative time of the day and try to work other less creative things around it, you'll no doubt get to ideas faster, get down more ideas and produce better work.

Don't assume that burning the midnight oil will always produce results — see *Late isn't always great*, page 75, for more.

IDEAS ABOUT CREATING IDEAS

Keep a bottom drawer
of your best unsold ideas

The good news is you will have hundreds of ideas in your career and lifetime. The bad news is that not all of those ideas will come to fruition. But, don't worry, more good news is on the way.

It's useful to keep your best unused ideas in a metaphorical bottom drawer: a place to fill with ideas that, for one reason or another, didn't see the light of day. It could be that you had a great idea that wasn't bought by the client. Or you had an idea that felt like it arrived too early for the client and to use it now would push them too far or require a budget that is not there.

Slowly, over the course of your career, your bottom drawer will fill up with some great ideas that are just waiting for the right client or the right moment to make them happen. This drawer not only keeps your ideas from dying but also becomes a place for you to pull from when you get the right opportunity in a brief. And sometimes revisiting old ideas after leaving them for a while can result in you using your additional experience to make them even better.

Utilise your best ideas, even if it's not immediately — see *If you have the idea, you can make it happen*, on page 89.

IDEAS ABOUT CREATING IDEAS

DON'T KNOCK OTHER WORK

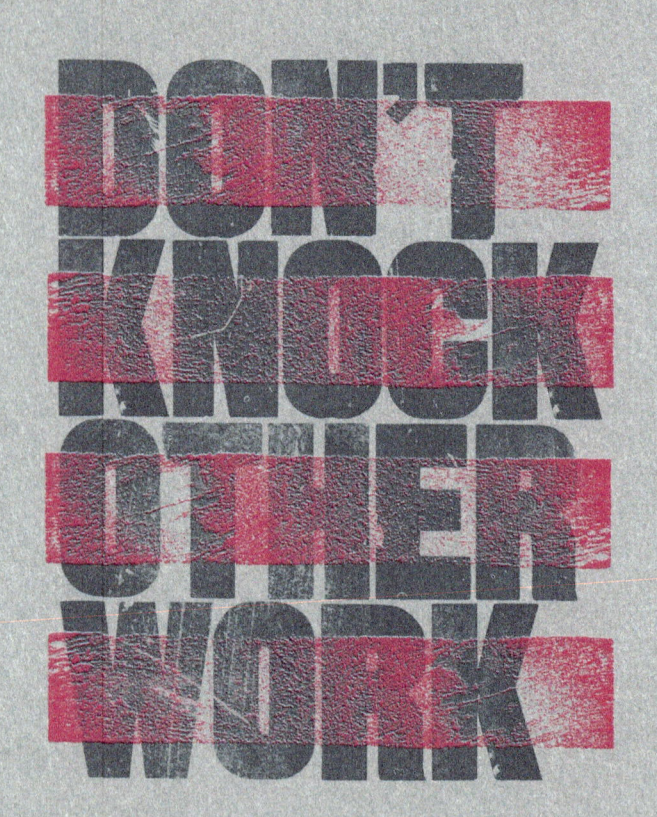

Creatives constantly look at other people's work. We can't help it. We love what we do and we want to be surprised by new ideas and ways of doing things that we haven't thought of. Great work not only inspires us but challenges us to be better.

But sometimes you'll see work that you feel could be stronger. It doesn't quite hit the mark, and if you were to work on that brief you would have made something better. The temptation is to knock the work and call it out as not being very good.

Don't... or, at least, be constructive.

Creating ideas all day can be tough. Add to that any restrictions such as:

- A tight deadline
- Little to no budget
- A client who wants to put their stamp on the work and make changes that weaken it
- A stakeholder who reacts to the work, but isn't aware of the brief or purpose
- A legal team who remove something human in favour of something more technical.

All of this (and more) has an impact on the quality of the final outcome.

So, when you're only seeing someone else's finished piece and don't know the behind-the-scenes story of how it was made, be sympathetic. Creative people take enough knocks when making work.

We all have work out in the world that wasn't quite as we first envisioned. Let's stay positive and build each other up.

Focus on your own work and success will follow. See *Don't judge yourself by others' success*, on page 113, for advice.

IDEAS ABOUT CREATING IDEAS

Time
OFF
is as important as time
ON

As a creative person, your brain will always be on. If you're ambitious, you will no doubt throw yourself into your work and want to keep producing ideas, to improve, to perhaps chase a promotion, and hopefully to work hard for the love of it.

But you must always remember to give yourself a break.

Time away from concentrating to think of ideas is as important as turning up every day to get the work done. It can actually help you to get the results you're trying so hard to achieve.

The solution to a problem often comes in the moments when we're not trying to think about it. That's why many people talk about getting great ideas on the loo or in the shower. Maybe there's something magical about bathrooms, or maybe it's because you're giving your brain a little rest and allowing some room for inspiration to strike.

Think beyond the bathroom and the likelihood is that, away from the workplace, your time will be spent living your life: going to a show, cheering on your team, visiting that place you've always wanted to, carving out some time to read (like you are now). All of these things will provide you with experiences and observations that you can pull from when you're next sitting down to think.

So make sure you and your ideas stay fresh with regular time out.

But what do you do on your days off? See *A connected creative hobby can unlock your mind*, on page 121, for ideas.

IDEAS ABOUT CREATING IDEAS

Start with writing

If you're a writer, feel free to flick to another tip*: you have this covered. If you're a designer, art director or any other creative responsible for visuals, read on. Words are powerful.

We tend to think and communicate in words more than pictures. Even if we have a visual idea, we often describe it to someone so they can have the picture in their mind too. When reading books, the words build pictures in our minds. If I talk about a monkey wearing a Superman outfit and riding on the back of a corgi, you now have the picture in your head. Albeit with your own monkey, your own corgi but possibly the same Superman outfit.

For more about getting down your ideas, see *Create first, edit later*, on page 31.

When creating visuals as part of a communication, we also need to consider what the visual needs to say. And it can be helpful to bring this to life in words before we leap into showing it as an image.

Before you do anything visual, try building a world of words first. Write down what you need to get across to your audience. Describe how an image or design should make people feel. Write individual attributes. Should it be scary? Sophisticated? Sensual? How should it move? What's the mood you're trying to convey? What's the story you have to tell? Is there a headline it needs to work with? If so, what does it say and how can the image complement it?

Getting all this down in words will not only help the ideas come out faster, but will also give you a point of focus for your visuals. Get the words right and you'll have something to bring to life in pictures.

Particularly if you're in a bookshop and you've magically opened the book at this point — there's more stuff in here for you, I promise.

IDEAS ABOUT CREATING IDEAS

DO
MORE
OF
WHAT
MAKES
YOU
GIGGLE

Creativity is the most powerful force in the world. It connects us, moves us and even makes giant leaps possible.

If you have created anything in your life, you would have felt the power of your own creativity. The moment when you went from a blank sheet of paper (literally or metaphorically) to something. It will no doubt cause a reaction in you. A surprise and delight that you – *you* – have made that.

For me, that feeling is a giggle. When I have created something that, moments before, didn't exist or came to life outside of my head and onto the page, I often audibly giggle. A true LOL. It's that feeling that keeps me coming back. It's addictive, a great source of joy – free joy – and there's nothing like it.

Not all of the creative jobs you work on will have this effect. But it's there. If it's not in your day job, you'll find it in other places like personal projects or things that you've never tried before. The power is within you to make it happen.

Make sure that your creative life is full of giggles (or whatever version of 'the giggle' you experience). Seek them out; they're often a sign that you've hit upon something special, or – at the very least – you're enjoying yourself.

Learn more about being guided by your feelings – see *F*ck likes, do what you love*, on page 115.

IDEAS ABOUT CREATING IDEAS

CREATE F1RST, EDIT LATER

When you're in the process of creating, there can be a tendency to judge your ideas as they come out. It's natural to question them and consider whether they're good or not. But the editing mindset is different to the creating mindset.

When you're creating, give yourself permission to let ideas flow without questioning their worth too much – at least not at this stage. You'll want to give yourself the chance to get down as many ideas as possible, so you can go from first ideas, which can be more obvious, to additional ideas, which can be more interesting and possibly unlock things that haven't been done before.

Once you have plenty of ideas down, then you can look to edit them. I say edit, but what you want to do is use a more positive mindset to improve on them. Rather than discount ideas, first question how they could be better: 'What if we added this?' 'What if we removed that?'

If the next stage of your process is to review the ideas with a creative director, don't edit too much by removing things you feel aren't good. We can feel the need to quickly hide ideas we don't like, as if we're ashamed of them, but sometimes ideas need a fresh or experienced view that could be the difference between the idea not being seen at all and being brilliant.

Don't be too harsh or hasty. Give your early ideas a chance to breathe; they may grow into your best.

See *Use the overnight test*, page 99, to get advice about spotting the really great ideas.

IDEAS ABOUT CREATING IDEAS

Write down ideas when they happen

Ideas have a habit of creeping up on you when you least expect them. Your job is to catch them before they completely disappear. The very second you have an 'aha!' moment, avoid an 'uh-oh!' by writing down your idea.

It doesn't matter how you do it. Keep a notepad and pen by your side. Record a voice memo or make a note on your phone. Scratch it into the table with a fork. Steal a passing child's crayons and schoolbook. Whatever your method, make sure you're always well equipped.

If you do decide to keep notebooks, take time to go through them and revisit old ideas. This is always time well spent as they often contain thoughts that you might not even feel like you wrote, but you did.

There may be a moment when you have an idea that you feel is so good, you will convince yourself that it's impossible to forget. Particularly late at night in bed, you think you'll definitely remember this one in the morning.

This is a trap.

In the same way that you can easily forget where your keys are, why you popped upstairs in the first place or what on earth possessed you to buy and wear a shell suit, ideas can leave you as quickly as they arrive. This only increases as you get older, trust me.

When you have ideas, grab them with both hands. Keep them. Hold them dearly. You never know when you might need them.

Read more about how great ideas are often born from many thoughts, with *Quality follows quantity*, on page 91.

IDEAS ABOUT CREATING IDEAS

BE KIND

TO YOURSELF
:)

If having an idea in the first place isn't tough enough, getting it made can be even tougher. There are plenty of battles to fight in the quest for great work:

- Translating the idea into the right words, imagery or sounds
- Getting others to understand your idea's value
- Protecting your work from various people's opinions along the way
- Working to a budget that doesn't quite stretch
- Maybe all of the above, while keeping to a near-impossible deadline.

So, don't beat yourself up.

Give yourself some time out as often and regularly as you can. Recognise when things are out of your control (and only focus on the things you can influence). Get your negative energy out through exercise and sport (where you can legitimately punch and kick things, if you like). Create your ideal version of the work, if that helps you to get it out of your system and makes you happy.

Your mental health is more important than anything or anyone. As a creative, your brain is your greatest asset, so look after it.

Learn how listening to your inner voice can have a positive effect; see *Trust your gut*, on page 101, for more.

IDEAS ABOUT CREATING IDEAS

Keep it simple

I was tempted to leave this page blank beyond these three words, but feel I have to explain this, as keeping it simple is easier said than done.

The creative industry can be full of bullshit, jargon, processes, egos, trends, bloated briefs, too many stakeholders and other things that can complicate what should be relatively straightforward. There is a problem, and creativity is there to provide an answer, a way to overcome the problem and create a positive outcome that has an impact.

See beyond the layers of complexity that can fill each day. Discard any distractions. Keep focused on the problem you are solving and find ways to creatively overcome it using any useful insights you have. If you don't have a problem to solve, turn the ask in your brief into a problem. You'll find that your ideas will start to flow.

The more you can simplify things, the sharper your work will be.

When you are crafting your work, see if there is anything you can take away from what you're making that will maintain the idea:

- Fewer words to make things punchier
- A shorter time span to hold attention
- One strong visual (if you need a visual at all).

It's also likely that people will understand the power of the idea, too. When selling your work, if you can take it from a simple problem statement to a single sentence describing your idea, you will have more chance of getting your audience to see the power in your thinking.

Less is more.

A few words can work wonders. Check out *Explain the idea in one sentence*, on page 59.

IDEAS ABOUT CREATING IDEAS

INPUT is as important as **OUTPUT**

Creativity happens when thoughts collide to create a new idea or different way of doing something. The crafting or development of your ideas might draw upon different references of things you've seen, heard or experienced. So, it's important to allow yourself time to simply absorb other things.

Those things are often connected to our creative pursuit, like keeping up with the latest advertising, seeking out design trends or reviewing photographers' portfolios. But it's also good to spend time on seemingly unrelated things like reading poetry, people-watching at the coffee shop or hitting shuffle on your playlist and listening to whatever song pops up. (And I mean *listening* – no background music or skipping to the next track.)

Working this into your day can be very effective. Your brain will have moments of activity (creative output) and moments of bingeing on stuff (creative input) that will collect in the recesses of your mind to use when the time is right.

You can only vomit what you eat. And the more stuff you have as reference, the more likely it is that you'll create something surprising, different, interesting and innovative.

Read more about how finding the unexpected can lead to the unexpected. See *Learn everything you can about the subject in your brief*, on page 69.

DON'T EVER

think you're the finished article

You can't talk about creativity without also mentioning ego.

People often mistake ego for a creative person who shows passion and is therefore protective of their work. This usually happens when someone else is trying to change their work without any reasoning. But that's not an ego, that's just someone caring about what they've created.*

An ego is a different beast. You'll know when you meet someone with an ego — it will stand out like a sore cliché. It isn't nice to work with. An ego can be destructive to an entire creative department, not just other individuals, particularly if it comes in the form of a creative leader.

Thankfully, most creatives I have worked with and admire actually suffer from crippling self-doubt. It's a trait that seems to drive them. The work they produce is actually incredible — if only they would realise it a little more often.

Let your work do the talking. Remember, there are always new things to learn. And stay curious — curiosity is one of the most creatively valuable traits you can have.

For more advice about how curiosity can keep the ego at bay, see *Never stop learning*, on page 57.

---

* *Which is a good thing if you don't fly off the handle and look like a dick**.*
** *Bonus tip: don't be a dick.*

IDEAS ABOUT CREATING IDEAS

WORK WITH THOSE WHO DO WHAT YOU CAN'T

Knowing your strengths can give you an advantage throughout your career, but understanding your weaknesses can also lead to good results. It takes a team of people to create great work, so knowing what you're not good at and collaborating with those who do what you can't is a must.

We tend to gravitate towards people who just seem to 'get us', mostly because they're very similar to us, but the strongest creative teams are diverse. A diversity of backgrounds and experiences brings a diversity of thought and ways of doing things that are key to creating work that resonates with others. It also increases the ability to develop innovative ideas or ways of working by bringing different (sometimes seemingly opposing or unconnected) things together to create something new.

> See *Don't knock other work*, on page 23, to see how different work can challenge us to be better.

The people you work well with may share the same work ethic and vision as you and the rest of the group, but actively seek out those who can effortlessly do the things that you struggle with. Spot them. Value them. When individuals bring their own unique superpower to the group, it can elevate the quality of the work to another level*.

This is especially important if it's your job to hire people and are responsible for building a team. You must look to bring in more of the difference rather than more of the same. Find a blend of complementing skills that can create a powerful creative force.

---

* See any of the actual superhero movies for evidence of this — nobody has the same skill, which is why they need to be a team.

**Done
is
better
than
PERFECT**

Creative people care about and have pride in what they make and how they make it. They spend time on their craft, honing their skills. Chasing perfection can be part of what drives them.

But beware!

Perfection can be something that puts a barrier in the way of creativity. A roundabout that can send you into a spiral, where you're never quite happy because you feel your work needs something more, that it can't be finished until that gap is filled.

Turn to *Leave room for happy accidents*, on page 87, to see how unplanned surprises can elevate your work.

Your life and career is one of constant improvement and progress. You may always seek to achieve something that requires a few more hours, months or projects under your belt.

Get your work to a place where it's as good as you can possibly make it and move on. It's more beneficial to your development as a creative to have something imperfect that's complete than to have an idea that's unmade because it's not quite perfect enough.

You will always take what you learnt from completing your last project and bring it into the next. It's part of your continual growth as a creative. The more work you produce, the more you'll learn and the better you'll get. And you can't learn anything until you've finished something.

When learning to paint, my instructor put it beautifully, advising: 'Your paintbrush contains a thousand bad paintings. It's your job as a student to get them out.'

IDEAS ABOUT CREATING IDEAS

A
WARDS
AREN'T EVERYTHING

There are endless award ceremonies in the creative industry. Hundreds of categories for all kinds of work with even more criteria for winning — from craft through to effectiveness.

Winning any award can be a boost to your confidence and your career. Pop up on stage to collect your gong (or several) during an evening, and you can guarantee that people from other companies will seek you out and probably offer you a new job while you're celebrating in the bar.

Winning an award can become all-consuming, though. I've seen creatives so fixated on it, they lose sight of what's right for the brief and problem at hand. Creative decisions become solely based on what they believe a judging panel might like. Sometimes they will even try and replicate previous winning work (theirs or someone else's) in the hope of finding the magic formula for success.

> Stuck for that award-winning idea? See *Keep a bottom drawer of your best unsold ideas*, on page 21, for some inspiration.

It's worth remembering that the distance between winning and not winning an award is so small you can slip a golden envelope through it. Awards can come down to a popularity contest, which isn't necessarily a sign of the best work (in the same way that a number-one single isn't an indicator of the best music out there).

So, if you do have something worthy of entering for an award, well done. If you get a nomination, take it as a win. And if you collect the trophy, take it gracefully with both hands (and the career move if it's worth it) and move on to the next project.

Winning an award is a by-product of making something great. It will only happen if you have work that's worthy of winning something. So focus on producing the best work you can, and anything else that happens is a bonus.

USE YOUR CREATIVITY

BEYOND YOUR DAY JOB

If you're lucky enough to be creative for a living — whether you're a designer, writer, photographer, art director or other — you will no doubt pour your heart into your daily work, particularly if you're looking to move up the ladder in an agency or to maintain your reputation as a freelancer (as well as pay your bills).

But when creating ideas for brands and businesses every day, it's also important to leave some space and energy for projects that are for yourself. Creativity that is free from the gauntlet of client approvals, brand constraints and keeping the legal team happy.

> Not all creative opportunities are equal, as *Some work feeds your bank account, other work feeds your soul*, on page 131, explains.

This could be writing a novel, glass-blowing an ornament, photographing a local team of hockey players, digging out your old watercolour set or stitching a tapestry — whatever you feel the creative urge to explore.

A personal project can be the perfect tonic to keep your creativity in balance when some of the challenges of delivering work for your day job can have a negative effect on how you feel, both creatively and in your general mental well-being.

Personal projects don't just have the power to feed your soul; they can also teach you a whole new skill, influence your day job in ways you never imagined, turn into a lucrative side hustle, become your most powerful work or even your very own business.

<u>Never forget this</u> and don't leave it until it's too late. Make sure you're always giving yourself the chance to do something for you.

IDEAS ABOUT CREATING IDEAS

Nobody can

SELL YOUR WORK

like you can

Creating the work is only half the battle of getting it realised and out into the world. Once made, it will need to be shared (and sold) to clients. Nobody can do this better than you, the person who made it.

Standing up in a room full of people and talking through your work can be a situation a lot of creatives will run from. But presenting your work yourself can make all the difference in getting it sold and keeping its integrity. If someone challenges your work, you will be able to respond to problems from a creative point of view, rather than just agreeing to any suggestion that's made in the room in the hope that the client will buy the work.

See *Selling the idea is as important as having the idea*, on page 103, for more selling tips.

If the idea of presenting scares you, think of the alternative: someone who didn't have the idea talking about your work:

- Would they be able to set up your idea before revealing the work?
- Would they be able to focus everyone on how the creative solution solves the problem?
- Would they be able to talk through the details and why they're there?
- Would they have the energy and enthusiasm for the work?
- Would they defend your work if the client tried to take it in a new direction?

Handing over your work for someone else to present can be a whole lot scarier.

Sure, there are people who are great at selling, but nobody else will have your understanding, your craftsmanship, your energy, your ability to fight for your work — so get yourself in that room.

You never know, you might actually enjoy it.

IDEAS ABOUT CREATING IDEAS

EVERY BODY'S MAKING IT UP AS THEY GO ALONG

When I started out in advertising, I wanted to learn all I could about how the industry worked, to peek behind the curtain in the hope that it would help me to navigate a successful career.

In my first role, I absorbed everything I could. I think I barely spoke for two years as I was busy watching everyone else and soaking up all the information. Once I cracked the code, I worked hard and got a few promotions. But when I moved to other agencies, I found that they did things differently and I had to learn all over again.

Once I got to the level of creative director and then executive creative director, I realised that the answers to how it all worked at the agency were now down to me. I used my previous experiences — picking what I felt were the best and most effective parts — to lead the way for my team and the agency. Other people in the leadership team would do the same. Sometimes there would be things none of us had experienced, or someone in the team might come up with a better way forward.

In short, everyone was making it up.

There is no right or wrong way to go about making creative work. You will find principles, techniques and tips along the way. There are a lot of them in this book. But this book is just a reflection of my experience and what has worked for me. It's your job to pick up as much advice as you can and decide what works for you.

Every project presents a learning challenge. See *What worked this time won't always work next time*, on page 79, for more.

IDEAS ABOUT CREATING IDEAS

Know your

SUPER POWER

Each one of us has a superpower, something we have a natural affinity with. It's not a talent as such, but it's part of how you operate. It's not just what you do, but *how* you do it.

Although creativity is a collective superpower, your individual superpower is likely to be something else: something that aids your creativity in some way.

My superpower is the ability to simplify things — to cut through everything that's superfluous and focus on what's important. This helps me to process creative briefs and make sure my work is direct. It has also come into its own when I'm leading teams.

Other superpowers include the ability to:

- Make connections between people or things
- Empathise with others
- Know what someone means, despite what they say
- Charm others and get them onside
- Keep calm and stay positive during tough times
- Sell the work to the client before you've even made it to the meeting room.

The list is endless. The likelihood is you have one power that rises above all the others.

You might not immediately know what your superpower is, but we all have one. Give it time and you will find out, or you can always ask people what they think. People are good at spotting the superpowers of others, as it's usually at the heart of why they value that person.

Once you are clear on what your superpower is, use it to great effect and collaborate with other people who have complementary superpowers to create an unstoppable team.

Knowing what you need help with is also key to success, as *Work with those who do what you can't*, on page 43, explains.

NEVER STOP LEARNING

One of the joys of having a creative mind is being curious about the world we live in. Questioning why things are a certain way. Trying to understand how things work so we can improve ourselves and look to make things better through our creativity.

There is always so much to learn with every project:

- A new subject to work with
- A new problem to solve
- New people to work alongside
- New technology that can make an idea possible
- New media, techniques and ways to bring the idea to life.

Even if a project fails, you will have learnt something from the experience that will help improve your next project.

Curiosity is a path to joy that you should enjoy wandering down. This should never leave you, no matter how long you have made a successful living by being creative or how many years ago you finished your formal education. Every day is a school day.

Read books, sign up for workshops, take online lessons, go to events, observe others... aim to learn something new every day and nourish your brain. It's your sense of wonder that keeps your mind playful and your creative output fresh.

You can learn something even when it all goes wrong. See *Failure is your best teacher*, page 137, to be inspired.

Explain the idea in one sentence.
Explain the idea in one sentence.
Explain the idea in one sentence.
Explain the idea in one sentence.
Explain the idea in one sentence.
Explain the idea in one sentence.
Explain the idea in one sentence.
Explain the idea in one sentence.
Explain the idea in one sentence.
Explain the idea in one sentence.
Explain the idea in one sentence.
Explain the idea in one sentence.
Explain the idea in one sentence.
Explain the idea in one sentence.
Explain the idea in one sentence.
Explain the idea in one sentence.
Explain the idea in one sentence.
Explain the idea in one sentence.
Explain the idea in one sentence.
Explain the idea in one sentence.
Explain the idea in one sentence.
Explain the idea in one sentence.
Explain the idea in one sentence.

As creatives, we can spend so much of our time on creating the idea, we forget how to explain it to people.

I don't mean a full, detailed explanation or a deck of slides to set things up; I'm talking about just one simple sentence so everyone is clear on what the idea is. Even you.

When you have an idea, think about how you would describe it to someone. How would you introduce the idea to them before revealing it? A good place to start is to sum up the business problem in a sentence; then your one line outlining the idea should be the answer.

> See *Write down ideas when they happen*, on page 33, for more on capturing your thoughts.

When you have crafted the perfect sentence for your idea, it will work to your advantage in a number of ways. The creative director will get what you're trying to do and can help build the idea. You can play with the execution of that idea and how you're bringing it to life in words and images without losing what the idea is. The rest of your team will understand the power of the idea and can get behind it, even explaining it to other people in your words rather than making up what they think the idea is. And lastly, your client will simply understand your solution to their problem (and even share it with other people in their business who weren't at the creative presentation). It sadly doesn't guarantee they will buy it, but it will definitely help you sell the work and make sure everyone is on the same page.

So to sum up in one sentence: when you're crafting your ideas, don't forget to craft a one-line explanation and you'll get better results.

FIND YOUR PEOPLE

Being creative is a wonderful feeling that can lead to incredible things. Collaborate with the right kinds of people and you can take your work to a new level and create great work more frequently.

How do you know when someone would be a good collaborator? There are three simple steps.

1. Admire their work from afar.
   The first step is the easiest. You'll know whether what they produce excites you and can influence your work in a positive way from simply looking at their portfolio. You'll no doubt have a mutual love of similar things, which will shine through in what you both make or want to make.

2. Meet people and speak to them.
   You'll need to have a good working relationship, so make sure you feel you could work together, as this isn't always the case or something you can tell from their work. The first clue to someone being right for you is that they're easy to talk to. Like most friendships, we have a good sense of people who just seem to 'get' us, and the same is true of good collaborators. Things will easily click and you'll feed off of each other's energy.

3. Work on something together.
   The true measure of a good collaborator is to try out the theory and work on a project. Or maybe even two or three. It won't always be plain sailing, but like all good relationships, you'll know if you're good for each other or not pretty quickly. And it's ok if you're not. The next partnership might be the one.

The process of finding your people can take a while, but your contact list of good collaborators will grow over time. And you'll find that, as you connect with your kind of people, they will have their own list full of other like-minded people that could work well with you, too.

For more on the importance of connecting with others, see *Bring people on your journey*, on page 97.

MASTER THE ART

not the software

From books and workshops to online lessons (or even a quick online search to find a specific answer you're looking for), there are many ways to keep improving your skills.

When looking online or browsing social media, you will be bombarded by 'influencers' teaching you simple, smart tricks, with a view to gaining followers and potentially selling you a course to take your learning further.

While it's great to know a trick or two, be mindful that a majority of these posts will teach you how to use software, particularly in the world of design. But if you want to improve your work, focus on mastering your craft:

- Learn the principles of design, not just Affinity Designer.
- Learn about human behaviour, not just Figma.
- Learn the psychology of colour, not just Procreate.
- Learn how light and shade works, not just Adobe Photoshop.
- Learn about how to tell a story, not just Final Cut Pro.

Prioritising the <u>why</u> over the how will not only improve your work, but it will also increase your value as a creative.

For some inspiration on mastering your craft, see *Make every element of your execution express your idea*, page 117.

Borrow & steal, but

NEVER
COPY

Looking at other creatives' work is part of the thinking process that makes our brains tick. We constantly leap from inspiration to creation. And creative work that feeds our minds will have an impact on our own creative output.

Musicians and singers tend to be a good indicator of this. You can often spot the artists who inspire them and influence the way they sing, perform or even dress. It can be a sign of their tastes, and also their knowledge and appreciation of other great work. Sometimes, they don't even try to hide it. (Oasis have always talked about their key inspiration being The Beatles, for example).

But you must be careful not to be so infatuated with a particular piece of work that you simply replicate it. Not only is there likely to be some kind of legal infringement, but you're also not adding anything of yourself to create something new. With most creatives attuned to other work that's out there, you'll get called out for copying too.

Be like a skilled chef. Take an ingredient from here and a technique from there and build a brand-new dish, or deliver something in a way nobody has experienced before. Continually seek out and collect as many influences as possible from your own experiences and connect the dots in a way that only you can.

What you absorb can make a difference to your own work, see *Input is as important as output*, on page 39, for more.

NO

DON'T LET THE WORD 'NO' GET TO YOU

When you work for a creative agency, your job is to generate ideas every day you turn up for work. Five days a week, fifty-two weeks a year, for however many years you decide to stay around. That's a lot of ideas.

You will be tasked with sharing those ideas with a creative director who (if they're good) will help you to shape a handful to share with the client. The client will then (if they're good too) choose one of those ideas and this is what will be made.

All that work for one idea. The idea that the client and everyone else said 'yes' to.

When sharing ideas, for every 'yes', you will hear the word 'no' several times more. Over time, this can be draining. It can break through the armour of even the most battle-worn creative.

A 'no' is never nice to hear. If it's a 'soft no' (in other words, if there's one thing getting in the way of it becoming a 'yes'), you might be able to find a creative way to fix the problem. But if it's a 'hard no' (and for whatever reason the idea is a no-go), remind yourself of the yesses that you've had along the way.

During your career, the noes will always outweigh the yesses. But the more noes you get, the more yesses you will be likely to hear.

Read *Don't present anything you don't want your client to choose*, page 17, for advice on how to keep things positive.

IDEAS ABOUT CREATING IDEAS

Learn everything you can about the subject in your brief

One of the joys of working on projects for a range of brands is the variety of problems and subject matter each brief provides. You could be trying to understand what makes a mother choose a certain brand of milk for her newborn one minute, then persuading a beer drinker to choose an authentic hand-crafted rum cocktail the next.

When you receive a brief, there can be a tendency to jump directly into what you feel the answer might be. This is no bad place to start, but you can add another dimension to your work if you get under the skin of your subject matter first. Really dive into the subject at the heart of your project.

If you're working on a brief for a chocolate bar:

- Eat it... smell it... blindfold yourself and <u>really</u> taste it. Do a taste test with similar products.
- Go to the factory and see how it's made.
- Ask why it's the shape it is.
- Ask where the name comes from.
- Find out about the evolution of the packaging design and what materials are used.
- Research where the ingredients come from and learn about those places.

The more you learn, the more you'll have to play with when it comes time to create ideas. Approach each subject with curiosity and wonder (even if it's a product or service you don't personally like, try to experience it as your audience would).

Find the joy in your subject and bring this into your work — it will be all the better for it.

Knowing nothing can be an inspiring place for a curious mind. See *No question is too stupid*, on page 15, for more.

IDEAS ABOUT CREATING IDEAS

The closer you are to
CLIENTS,
the closer you are to
SUCCESS

In the past, the world of commercial creativity relied on two aspects:

1. The creative part, the focus of 'creative people' who were responsible for the creative work.
2. The commercial part, undertaken by 'account people', tasked with selling the ideas to the clients and handling the business side of things.

It's now more common for the creative team (not just the creative director) to have a direct connection with the client. If the thought of that makes you want to run away...

Firstly, there's nothing to be afraid of. Clients are people (that often want to make great work) too.

Secondly, clients are paying for your expertise; they want and need your skills, so you're already off on the right foot.

I would go as far as to say that, when a client has the chance to talk directly to someone in the creative team, it's the highlight of their day. They can loosen the tie of their corporate day-to-day and connect with someone who can seemingly perform magic that can help their business.

So, make sure you get the chance to connect with your client, whether this is at the beginning of the briefing stage or when it comes time to presenting work – from inception to completion. When you have a direct connection with them, you will have the chance to gain their confidence in your abilities and in the work itself. It's also easier to protect your work as it goes through the various stages of approval on its way to being made.

The stronger this connection is, the more likely you are to be trusted, and your work will have more chance of maintaining your vision.

For more on why client connection is important, see *Nobody can sell your work like you can*, on page 51.

IDEAS ABOUT CREATING IDEAS

BUILD YOUR HAPPY PLACE

Working in the right environment can boost your creativity in the same way the right song coming through your headphones can transform your jog into a personal best or turn a walk down the street into more of a strut (you do that too, right?).

With a majority of creative agencies adopting an open-plan office culture, this can be quite challenging. Being creative can easily feel like a desk job (which it isn't) and you're open to all kinds of interruptions that can stop your ideas dead in their tracks.

Sometimes less is more. See *Keep it simple*, on page 37, to find out why.

You will have no doubt found your perfect creative haven in the form of a pub or coffee shop to combat this, but with hybrid working now more common, take a look at your creative space away from the office and turn it into the perfect place to inspire your ideas.

You could be lucky enough to have a whole room or maybe it's just a corner in your flat, but consider everything that surrounds you to set the right tone. Think about the music you play or whether noise-cancelling headphones will help you achieve pure silence; the art you have on the walls; what colour you paint the walls; whether there's a window you can people-watch from; what smells uplift you or transport you somewhere otherworldly; a selection of stationery including your favourite fancy wooden pencils with an elaborate sharpener. Perhaps there's a shelf full of your favourite books within hand's reach. Maybe you include this one, then decide to buy one for a friend and write a positive review on Amazon.

Create the environment that makes you feel inspired and ready for ideas. A place where you're free to think without judgement. A place that's an extension of your mind, if not an extension on your actual home.

LATE
isn't always
GREAT

The culture of working late nights is rife in the creative industry, particularly in advertising agencies. Especially when there's a new business pitch. You're trying your best to work with the little time that you have, and any additional hours are seen as helpful.

But regularly working for an extended period of time doesn't always lead to great creative work. Thinking is often better in short, concentrated bursts. If you sit and think twice as long, you won't necessarily produce double the quantity of work — or have work that's twice as good.

Creativity needs time for reflection, time away from the problem and time to feed the brain (with inspiration — not free beer and pizza), so it's not running on empty.

Give yourself pockets of time away and you will no doubt happen upon something you won't have considered by sitting at your desk into the wee hours. Allow yourself space to see things differently. It's in these moments that an idea can often creep up on you without warning while you're doing something else.

When it comes to your creative reputation, you'll be judged on the quality of your work, so give yourself the best chance to create great work.

—
Doing nothing can sometimes add something to the work. See *Time off is as important as time on*, page 25, for more.

IDEAS ABOUT CREATING IDEAS

KNOW WHEN TO STOP

When learning how to ride a bike, people tend to focus on the riding part — it's not until you're wobbling along, trying to not fall off, that you wish someone would have told you more about the stopping part.

Creativity is quite similar. Knowing how and when to stop is key. You won't scrape your knees if you don't, but you might overproduce the work and lose the magic.

A surefire way to know if you're tinkering is that you start to add things. Instead, focus on what can be taken away. Questioning how you can make the work simpler while maintaining the idea will lead to more refined work that's easier and quicker for the audience to get and therefore more effective.

You may also find yourself staring at the same piece of work, wondering if there's something you, or the work, is missing. If, despite your best efforts, it doesn't come to you, the chances are it's complete. It's a good idea to give yourself a time limit here or maybe walk away from the work for a while and use the overnight test (see page 99).

A good measure of when to stop is when you get 'the giggle' (see page 29 for more). If your own idea or a finishing touch delights you, it's likely to have the same effect on others, so don't lose this power by making unnecessary changes.

Sometimes, usually when putting together your portfolio, you can look at an old project with fresh, more experienced eyes and decide to make some improvements. Don't. Move on. It's good that your portfolio shows growth. Stop wasting creative energy on the past and pour your experience into what you make next.

Got the idea? Good, I'll stop there.

See *Present however many ideas are right for your problem*, page 129, to learn why doing too much work can work against you.

IDEAS ABOUT CREATING IDEAS

What worked this time ~~won't always work next time~~

When you have some creative success, it can be tempting to try to replicate it by taking the same approach for your next brief, pitch or project. If you're under pressure from deadlines, your instinct could even be to copy your past ideas to deliver something on time. But doing this could quickly earn you the reputation of a being a one-trick pony.

While there are some principles (as many as I can think of are in this book), there is no real formula for success when it comes to creating great work. What won the pitch, scooped the award or got your work past the creative director last time won't always be the right thing to do again.

For advice on keeping your approach fresh, check out *There is always another way*, on page 111.

If you're struggling with your work and want a different outcome, you'll need a new approach.

A good starting point is to literally do the opposite of what you are currently doing. Turn your idea, point of view or ritual on its head.

Can't think of a good solution? Think of as many bad examples as you can and then turn them into positive ones.

Can't get the right simple visual? Write about it using as many words as possible.

Usually start with scribbling down ideas? Carefully craft a sentence outlining what the problem is.

Get yourself out of your habits and instincts to surprise and delight yourself. Trick yourself into seeing things from a different angle, refreshing and resetting the brain.

Leave your comfort zone and you could develop a fresh approach or idea that you've never thought of before.

Look after your mind:
it's your greatest asset

From the outside, creative people can seem to have an endless stream of ideas that pour from their very being for the world to see and enjoy. In reality, if you work in the creative industry, it's very different.

New technology means deadlines are getting shorter. Budgets can be greatly reduced and clients only spend money on work that they believe will give them the greatest return on their investment. The internet provides a lot of exposure to ideas that have already been made, putting pressure on creative people to come up with something new. All of this can take its toll on your mind.

—
Your mind is valuable to yourself and others, see *Know your worth*, on page 153, for more.

You may not notice at first, but the thrill of winning pitches and awards, chasing a promotion, beating last year's campaign, delivering something wonderful for a super-tight deadline, maintaining your reputation with more brilliant work... all of it chips away at your mental health.

You must give yourself time away from the pressures of work and, most importantly, have a mental break. This can often be difficult for creative minds who like to be busy — you can't simply turn the tap off — but I urge you to find ways to give your brain some space to rest and recover.

Creative pursuits like craft projects or painting (two personal favourites) are activities that provide the creative output you enjoy but enable your brain to work in an almost meditative way. Things like fishing and hiking are also good for achieving something but switching off.

Then, of course, there is learning the art of actual meditation. A chance to understand more about how your brain works, connect with your feelings and be more present throughout everyday life.

IDEAS ABOUT CREATING IDEAS

SEE EVERY PROBLEM AS A CREATIVE OPPORTUNITY

The creative industry isn't perfect. There can be many frustrating things that get in the way of creating great work. These barriers and frustrations can be annoying and can take the shine off what is a wonderful way to make a living. As a person who is attuned to problems, they can get you down and, over time, make you bitter.

I'm not going to say 'stay positive and get over it', but what I will say is that you're a person who is valued because you can take problems and turn them into solutions. The same can be applied to many aspects of the problems you come across on the job.

> Problems don't need to be a cause for concern, see *Don't panic!* on page 123 for advice on how to overcome them.

Don't like the way something is? Find and suggest a better way.

Don't think someone quite gets it? Devise ways to get them on board.

Believe someone has a problem with something? See it as a chance to help them.

A good director will help anyone in their team who is positively brimming with ideas. The whole team, however, will find it annoying to work with someone who is a bit of a perpetual moaner.

It's fine to call stuff out and get things off your chest. But whenever there is a problem, see it as an opportunity waiting to happen. You won't always be able to change everything, but suggest new ideas and ways of working.

Maintain a can-do attitude and, more often than not, you can change things for the better.

IDEAS ABOUT CREATING IDEAS

Be your own
HYPE MAN*

*This reference is purely down to my love of hip-hop, please feel free to amend to suit your gender.

Creative people can be perceived as outgoing extroverts who like to be the centre of attention and the life and soul of the party. If this sounds like you, you can skip this tip, but if you're one of the quiet, introverted types who likes to skirt around the edges of the party (or not go in the first place), this one's for you.

Make sure you have a good online presence with an up-to-date portfolio (that works well across all devices). This is a must. You'll be surprised how many people don't have this, so completing this basic step will set you ahead of the others.

Thankfully, social media helps those who feel awkward in real-life social situations. Your socials don't have to be a constant stream of self-promotion (although that's no bad thing), but make sure you're joining in with other conversations. Make it part of your daily routine and see it as a chance to get creative.

Recruiters spend their time looking on LinkedIn for good candidates. Make this part of your social media world and share updates here often. Being front of mind with recruiters is important, as they'll easily forget you.

Finally, try to get yourself out there in the real world. There are plenty of creative events happening near you: award ceremonies, talks, workshops, writers' groups and smaller gatherings.

It can be anxiety-inducing at times, but to be a success in the creative industry, people need to know about you, your expertise and what you can offer. You don't need to become loud or change your personality, but you may need to work a little harder to put yourself and your work in the minds of other people.

For more on getting yourself out there, see *Network beyond where you work*, on page 133.

Leave room for happy accidents

Not everything you do will go to plan. This is OK. It can even be an advantage if you let it. Mistakes can sometimes offer surprises that turn out well and make the work better – happy accidents.

These moments tend to happen after you've had the idea and when you're making the work (particularly when you're in the production stages of a project and shooting photography or film). This is generally the most planned part of the creative process, but it can also offer the chance to elevate the work while you're making it.

———
Check out *Make improvements, not changes*, on page 127, to learn the key to enhancing your work.

It could be finding a more suitable prop while searching for something completely different; shooting in a place next to the location you thought would be perfect because the feel and light is better; or using an unexpected spell of bad weather to add some drama to a shot.

With productions, you always have to roll with some things you haven't planned for and make decisions on the fly. Go into them accepting this and use this knowledge to your advantage.

Plan everything and you'll come back with exactly what you expected. Leave five per cent for creativity and you could elevate the work beyond what you and everyone else expected.

If you have the

IDEA

you can make it happen

All creative people will, at some point in their career, have an idea for something they'd like to make — usually something that sits outside of their day job. It will come to you and get you excited about the possibilities, then keep coming back to you, nagging you until you make it happen.

It could be an idea for something that doesn't yet exist but technology can now make possible, the beginnings of a plot for a great novel, a documentary about a subject that inspires you and has a story that you want to tell, maybe even an idea nobody has created before and you can't believe they haven't.*

> Energy is key for getting your ideas off the ground. See *Energy and hard work beats talent*, on page 157, for more.

It could be that you need to make a prototype to test out your thinking and to bring your idea to life for other people. Google are great at this. Founders Larry Page and Sergey Brin tried out ideas at home to show how they could work, and from this both Google Books and Google Earth were born. Knowing the advantage of creating in this way, Google give everyone who works for them time in their schedule to go out and make things.

You don't have to work for Google to take this approach. Carve out some time to consider the bigger picture and develop some potential game-changing ideas, or simply listen to when good ideas come calling.

Whatever the idea and however (and whenever) it comes, don't wait for someone or something else. Give yourself some time to make it and then go and make it happen.

A lot of good ideas share this trait.

IDEAS ABOUT CREATING IDEAS

QUALITY *follows* QUANTITY

OK, so this is not true alphabetically, but when it comes to generating ideas, it is.

For every brilliant idea you have, there will be many that don't shine so brightly. But it doesn't mean they're not useful. Every thought you get down won't immediately be brilliant, but we all know what happens to ugly ducklings.*

Your initial focus is to get down as many ideas as possible. Not just a handful, but hundreds. Don't judge your thoughts. Don't overthink it. Just write. Challenge yourself to write non-stop for ten minutes at a time and see what comes out. It's better to write something bad (odd or repetitive) than to not write anything at all.

Read more about improving your craft — see *Master the art, not the software*, on page 63.

Essentially this is about throwing clay onto the potter's wheel before shaping it into a pot. The more clay you have, the more you have to work with and the more impressive the pot.

Not sure where to start?

- Rewrite the brief in your own words.
- Write about the product from the audience's point of view.
- Write about the benefits and what they could mean to people.
- Write why people buy it, why they don't.
- Consider the impact the product or service can have on people's lives.

You'll soon have hundreds of thoughts to connect, refine, build and shape into fewer, stronger ideas. When you do, keep it positive. Look to improve things that have something rather than dwell on the things that don't. Pull the quality from the quantity until you have a beautiful vase.

If you don't, email me; I'm not one for widespread spoiler alerts.

IDEAS ABOUT CREATING IDEAS

The perfect brief

DOESN'T EXIST

Creative people are obsessed with creative briefs.

'What's the brief?' is often the first question on their lips when talking about work. They anticipate a one-sentence reply. Some will refuse to work on a project until they get one. In writing.

And when they do, they expect the brief to be short — ideally on one page. They want it to be inspiring, with all the gems and none of the jargon. Something insightful that has the power to spark their imagination.

The reality is that most of your creative briefs won't be like this. If you wait for the perfect brief before you set out to produce that award-winning piece, the chances are, you never will.

If you look at award-winning work,* you'll notice that it's unlikely that it would have been born from a perfect creative brief. Of course, that's how it will come across in the case-study video, with the benefit of hindsight. We like to see a clear path from problem to solution. It tells a clear story, something that works wonders on a judging panel, but again, it's not the reality of how great work is really made.

If you want to make something great, don't wait for the ideal brief. Don't wait for anything. Get out there and make it happen yourself. Join meetings to learn about your clients' problems. Understand how the audience behaves. Seek the barriers that can be overcome by a creative thought. Notice something insightful that others miss during workshops and discussions. Be visionary.

The things that will spark truly great ideas are not written on a piece of paper. So if you want to create game-changing ideas, change the game.

See *The most inspiring thing isn't always on the brief*, page 109, for more about working on creative briefs.

---

*Not the work that's been made just for the awards.

IDEAS ABOUT CREATING IDEAS

DON'T WAIT
FOR YOUR IDEAS TO HAPPEN

If you're working in an agency, you'll be responding to client briefs that are booked into the studio for a set amount of time for you to work on, depending on the brief and budget. Once you've completed your work on a project, you'll move on to the next creative brief.

The downside to this way of working is that it can breed a culture where the creative department only leaps into action once it has been asked. You'll move from one brief to the next and wait until the next request comes your way.

If you want your ideas to see the light of day — and also be there to protect them along the way — the last thing you'll want to do is wait. The moments in between creating work are incredibly important — these can be the places where ideas die.

Be active. Follow up with people. Ask how the meeting went. Chase people to find out where the project is at and whether there's anything you can do to help it progress. Be interested in the project. Pester people to the point of annoying them. Be a creative nuisance.

Bring your energy to the team and help move things along. It can be the difference between an idea happening and being forgotten.

Learn more about how your behaviour can impact the work and your team. See *Be the spark*, on page 143.

IDEAS ABOUT CREATING IDEAS

BRING

PEOPLE

ON

YOUR

JOURNEY

When you're creating ideas, you aim to develop something that nobody has seen before. The challenge with creating something groundbreaking is that there is no point of reference for people to connect with. It's new territory.

Despite wanting to be seen as an innovative agency or client, there is nothing quite as scary to marketing and advertising people as something so new it doesn't come with the experience of the past or, even worse, a dead cert that it is going to work.

You'll hear a lot of people in the creative industry talk about 'being brave'. This type of bravery isn't really 'being brave' at all, it's just the opposite of playing it safe. Producing expected ideas, things we feel we've seen before.

The key to creating work that requires 'bravery' to make it happen is how you take people on the journey with you. You need to put extra effort into helping people understand your vision and why you believe it is worth taking a punt on.

It's likely you'll need to present a truly innovative idea differently. You may need to show some deeper insights before revealing it. You may want to bring in new departments or specialisms to help build out your thinking in more detail. You might connect your idea to a success story in a completely different sector. You could even make a prototype or a nearly finished piece so your idea or execution is unmistakably understood.

Don't underestimate the need to bring everyone on the journey with you on the path to making something that's never been done before. See things from other, often more sceptical, points of view and learn how you can reassure or excite people into taking a creative leap of faith that goes beyond expectations.

Ideas need the support of others to make them a reality. See *Even creative directors need a creative director*, on page 105, for more.

IDEAS ABOUT CREATING IDEAS

Use the

OVER-
NIGHT
TEST

The journey from problem to solution can be a bumpy road. We get excited as new ideas enter our heads, furiously scribbling them down before they fly away. Then we can have moments of doubt when those ideas are no longer new and we start to question whether they're actually any good.

In these moments, I like to adopt what I call the 'overnight test'. Essentially, it's giving yourself time away from the idea. Leaving an idea until tomorrow allows it to live for a while in the back of our minds. If it sticks there or continually comes back to us, it's often a sign that it's good, and it will do the same for your audience.

When you return to the idea the following morning, you have reset your brain with rest and will view it with a fresh pair of eyes. The idea could surprise and excite you once again. With this new energy, you can think of ways to improve the idea. You could also decide on reflection that the idea actually isn't working (and that's OK).

I adopt this method as much as my schedule allows and have it as a key part of my creative process. It can work wonders for your ideas, improving the better ones and leaving the rest.

If you can turn an 'overnight test' into an 'over the weekend test', even better.

Get advice on how to manage your timescales effectively — see *Know your most creative time of day*, on page 19.

IDEAS ABOUT CREATING IDEAS

TRUST YOUR GUT

This is a piece of advice that you've probably heard before and no doubt have used many times. It's relevant to a lot of situations in life and is also true when it comes to creativity. So I feel it deserves its place in this book.

You will have moments every day, which will continue throughout your career, where you will make a decision seemingly based purely on how you feel. You may not be able to articulate why your decision is good or bad or right or wrong, but deep down you can feel it.

This is your gut talking.

Not all of your decisions will be made with logic or reasoning and this is absolutely fine. Over time you will accumulate a lot of experience, advice and learning — all of which will feed your gut and help it to become a barometer for helping to make good (or avoid bad) decisions.

So when your gut speaks, listen.

Build on what your gut is telling you. See *Make a note of what works*, on page 159, for more.

Selling the idea is as important as having the idea

As a creative person, your focus will be on ideas. Having them, making them, learning from them. Ideas. Ideas. Ideas.

A big factor in making those ideas happen is your ability to sell them to other people, whether those people are clients, members of your team or even the person you're collaborating with.

I have witnessed great ideas being sold so badly that they confused the client and they therefore didn't buy into it. Equally, I have seen mediocre ideas being sold to a client in a way that delighted them so much, they not only bought the idea but also found more budget to make it happen.

Selling the idea is an art unto itself, a skill that is more than worth learning.

If you're not sure how to sell or feel uncomfortable talking in front of an audience, stay close to those who do. Ask to be in the room when work is being presented, either internally or to a client. Observe how ideas are shared with others. See how they tell a story and take people on a journey. Notice how people react to what's being said. Look for the moments where the audience (including you) nod their heads, smile and get excited by the idea.

In time, you will learn how to not just talk about your ideas but to sell them to people. You'll find your own way of doing it.

The most important thing is that you master the art as part of your craft.

See *Big ideas don't always need big budgets*, on page 151, for more tips on increasing your chances of your work becoming a reality.

Even
CREATIVE DIRECTORS
need a
CREATIVE DIRECTOR

For the majority of your career, you will have the support of a creative director (or executive creative director, chief creative officer or another such title). It's that person's job to help you create the best work you can.

But what happens when you are the creative director and there's nobody to mentor you?

The truth is, we all need somebody to share ideas with. Somebody who we trust, who we can work well with and who has the ability to give honest, constructive feedback that can help elevate an idea.

My creative director is my wife. It helps that she's also in the creative industry, but it works because she has the right balance of being on the same page as me but also bringing skills, thoughts and ideas that I don't have. She gets where I'm coming from but can also point out things I haven't considered.

When you reach the highest level in the agency, it's a good idea to find a 'creative director' with the right skills to fit you. They could be a peer at the agency, someone you have worked with previously or someone who is not in the industry at all.

When you find them, hold them dear. Marry them if you have a strong enough connection – I highly recommend it.

> What happens when someone turns down your ideas? See *Don't let the word 'no' get to you*, on page 67, for advice.

IDEAS ABOUT CREATING IDEAS

YOU

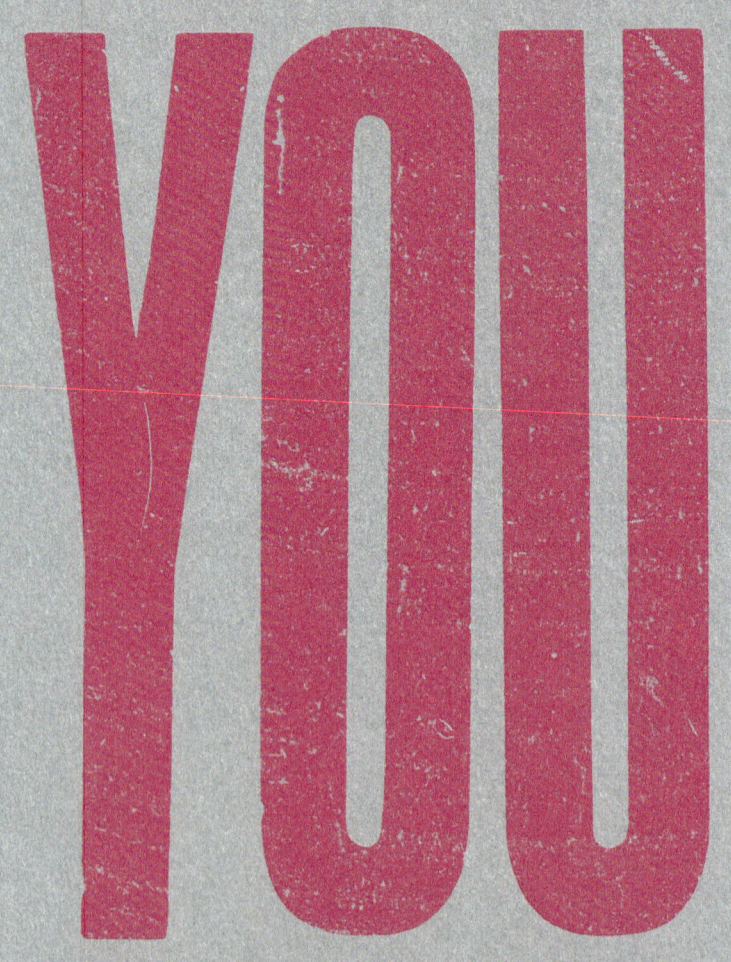

are not defined by your job title

Job titles can be simple, clear and help you understand someone's specialism — or your own. Copywriter, designer, art director, photographer, editor, animator... it's clear what the expertise of these roles are.

There are other job titles that seem to exist purely to give a sense of hierarchy or structure to an agency or studio — particularly if they have 'junior' or 'senior' attached to them. These additions are meaningless, but some people can become obsessed by them.

The truth is, they aren't a measure of who you are or, more importantly, what you can do. There are brilliant junior designers and not-so-good senior designers out there. The only thing that determines your worth as a creative is the work you produce and the way you go about it.

So, don't worry or get precious about what you're called. And don't go chasing a job title that's simply adding another word to what you are now. Just focus on creating the best work you can.

While we're on the subject of job titles, don't give yourself a handful of them on your website or CV either. You may have many talents, but if you class yourself as a designer, photographer and editor (I've seen five job titles on one CV before), you're making it hard for someone to understand your specialism. Remember, people looking for talent to join their team are generally looking to fill one role and are expecting that person to collaborate with others, not do it all themselves.

Let your work do the talking, not your title.

See *Know your superpower*, on page 55, for more on understanding your strengths.

IDEAS ABOUT CREATING IDEAS

The most inspiring thing isn't always

on
the
brief

The creative brief is the most important document in the agency. Of course, it's more than just a document, but the physical brief is the creative guiding light. It's the starting point for creative work and is also what you should refer back to when reviewing it.

A great creative brief should:

- Clearly state the problem to be solved
- Include who we're communicating to and what we want them to do
- Share something insightful about the product, service or audience
- Include some form of strategy
- Provide a clear point of difference and even some analysis on the competition.

But despite providing all this information, it still may not contain the thing that sparks your idea.

Armed with the knowledge that the brief provides, it is always worth doing some of your own research and exploration beyond the brief. This could be in collaboration with a member of the strategy or client team (asking them questions to dig deeper into a certain area) or simply searching online for more information.

You could find something interesting in the way the product is manufactured, maybe something about the brand's heritage or even a key insight from how the audience talks about or interacts with the brand on social media.

While you should never ignore the brief, give yourself the chance to find a gem that could spark your imagination and lead to an unexpected idea.

For more on cracking a brief, see *To think outside the box, make sure there's a box*, page 145.

THERE IS ALWAYS ANOTHER WAY

Coming up against barriers is all part of the job when it comes to creativity. There are many things that can get in the way of your ideas happening, including budget or time constraints, receiving some difficult or dramatic feedback, or simply because your client (or one of the many stakeholders) simply says 'no' to something.

At first, this can be frustrating. Your initial reaction can be to feel like a good idea has slipped by – another idea for the 'one that got away' pile.

But there is always another way.

Creativity thrives when faced with a problem. So when you hit a wall, treat this moment like a problem you need to overcome, and look at it from a different angle.

———
Turn to *See every problem as a creative opportunity*, page 83, for more advice on overcoming problems.

This could be getting to the heart of the reasoning behind a 'no' and seeing how this particular issue can be resolved. Or finding out if there's one part of the execution of the idea that could make it work. It could mean finding cheaper materials, making fewer assets, art-directing the work again, rewriting the copy to fit a particular tone, or coming up with another idea that avoids the issue that arose.

This can seem like the hardest thing when you have an idea that you felt was right, but sometimes coming at it from a different angle can result in something even stronger. It is difficult, but if you have the ability to see any barrier as a problem to overcome, you will elevate your creative thinking skills and also your value as a creative.

IDEAS ABOUT CREATING IDEAS

DON'T JUDGE YOURSELF BY OTHERS' SUCCESS

Whether you're watching the announcements of the winners from the Cannes Lions awards from the comfort of your laptop or scrolling through your feed to see that the designer you love has posted yet another amazing piece of work (their fourth that week), it can feel like others are winning while you're not doing so well.

Shift your focus away from other people. Forget about them and allow yourself to concentrate on you and the work you are producing. Your creative life and career will see plenty of ups and downs. Big wins, little setbacks. Your aim is to always move forward in some way.

—
Success is measured in many ways — see *Awards aren't everything*, on page 47.

Consider where you were a day, a week or a year ago, and compare this to where you are now. You may not notice, but you will improve and hone your craft the longer you do it and the more hours you put in (over time, not overtime).

Review what you've made. Or better still, keep a diary to help you track your progress. I guarantee what you're creating now is better than what's come before. There's probably someone looking at your work wishing they had done that.

So, be inspired by others but focus on your own work, and progress and success will follow.

F*CK LIKES

do what you love

Social media can be hashtag-amazing: offering you ways to promote yourself, connect with other people and see an endless feed of work that inspires you. It can also teach you how to open a bottle of wine with your armpit, show you families pulling off impressive dance moves and bring your attention to cats that look like celebrities.

I heartily recommend you use it, with one exception: don't let achieving likes and gaining an audience rule what you create or share.

Brands can fall into this trap. And they can easily lose sight of who they are, why they exist or what they stand for in the process. If you venture down this path, you can lose yourself too – second-guessing what people might find interesting and seeing yourself as a failure if you don't get the number of likes or comments you'd hoped for.

See social media and any gratification it provides as a bonus. Your creative life is a journey that should be guided by making things that you love, not what others might like. Follow this rule and it will be worth more than any following on any platform.

———
See *Use your creativity beyond your day job*, page 49, for more on how you can discover projects you'll love.

IDEAS ABOUT CREATING IDEAS

Make

every

element

of

your

execution

express

your

idea

You will make hundreds of decisions over the lifecycle of a project, but the choices I'm focusing on here purely relate to how your work is executed. It's mostly the art direction and design of a piece of work, but it can also be true of writing.

Whatever element you're crafting, you should always make sure every executional choice is made with the purpose of delivering the idea. Making choices because you think it 'looks good' isn't enough. This isn't about personal preference, it's about what's right for the idea.

Your typeface should reflect the tone of your message. The colours you choose should fit the tone of your idea, whether light, bright and uplifting or deep, dark and moody. The imagery should be shot in a way that not only connects you with the headline, but also has the right feel.

This is true of everything you put on the page or a screen.

If you have specific choices already made for you in the guise of brand guidelines, then look for the flexible opportunities that exist within them. Rules, after all, are made to be broken — or, at the very least, pushed to be purposeful.

When you do this, your idea will be much stronger for it as every part of the work has a reason for being. Everything has been considered, cared for and well crafted.

You will also find it easier to deal with subjective feedback, as, if something is called out for being not to someone else's taste, you can tell them why it's there and how it is a key part of expressing the idea.

—
See *Borrow and steal, but never copy*, on page 65, for more ideas on how you can learn tricks from other great work.

SAYING 'NO'
is no bad thing

It's not always a nice thing to hear, but sometimes 'no' is the right or only answer.

If you're a freelancer and have an opportunity that doesn't feel quite right or you're being asked for your rates to be dramatically reduced, it can be tempting to agree, but more powerful to say no. It may feel like an opportunity missed, particularly when things are quiet, but it's better for you in the long run as you don't want a reputation for just agreeing to everything.

During the process of creating work, some people fear telling a client 'no' and will try to avoid it, but ultimately clients pay for an agency's expertise. This should include calling things out when they don't seem right, particularly if it threatens any creative integrity, which will also impact the effectiveness of what you're making.

Your focus should be making decisions that will make the work better, not agreeing to what the client thinks they want in the hope that will make them happy.

If you need to push back on requests that could have a negative impact on your work, do this with a rationale and reasoning – reminding people about the purpose of the work and how it's a solution to the problem.

When you follow up a 'no' with a 'why', people will be more understanding, rather than it seeming like you're just being precious or awkward.

To push the boundaries, we sometimes need to push back and protect the work, but this only happens if you approach it in the right way at the right time. See saying 'no' as a positive thing that will result in stronger, more effective work.

It takes a strong leader to stand up for ideas. See *Leadership is a mindset, not a job title*, on page 147, for more on why that should be you.

A CONNECTED CREATIVE HOBBY CAN UNLOCK YOUR MIND

When you're lucky enough to have a job that allows you to be creative every day, you can put your all into it. But you will also find times when your mind is a little rusty and focused on other things or you just can't seem to conjure up the magic.

Everybody goes through this. It's all a part of being creative, especially if you're expected to deliver five days a week, fifty-two weeks a year.

There are plenty of things you can do to overcome creative block. But having a creative hobby that's connected to what you do in your day job can work wonders for reaching the far corners of your mind.

So, if you're a writer, do some painting. A film-maker? Write some poetry. Or if you're an art director, why not try some needlepoint?

The aim of the game here isn't to gravitate towards something you're good at (although you may get good at it over time), but to connect to another form of creative expression that's outside of your usual focus. Some creative activities can put you in an almost meditative state, which can unlock ideas. And you'll also produce another type of great creative work in the process.

Learn how doing nothing at all can sometimes help you. See *No day is wasted* on page 155.

DON'T PANIC!

Your emotions will change throughout the duration of the creative process.

At the start, there is usually excitement at the prospect of a new problem to get your grey matter working. This can be followed by the thrill of getting new ideas down onto the page.

Next up, you can expect a visit from the doubting side of your brain. The 'this is great' from yesterday can become today's 'this is shit'.

Every creative goes through this. You may not see it, as it's rarely on show, but even the best creative people have self-doubt. A lot of great creatives struggle with it.

It's easier said than done, but don't panic in the moments when you think your idea is shit. Or if you don't have any ideas at all. Worrying about your lack of output with a looming deadline is only going to take space up in your brain and may stop you from thinking anything at all.

Ideas rarely come out fully formed. They'll need work. So get something down — anything. Rewrite the brief in your own words. Or write a load of stupid ideas, if you like. Focus on filling the page with whatever you have in your head. Before long you'll then have something to work with: something to craft, shape and develop.

Do this and it just might turn out great.

Turn to page 27 for more tips on getting ideas down and how, when you *Start with writing*, you can kickstart your creativity.

IDEAS ABOUT CREATING IDEAS

REVIEW ROUGH THOUGHTS

present finished ideas

Throughout your career you will be required to share your ideas with a creative director, whose job it is to work with you to shape and refine your thinking.

You are likely to want to impress the creative director with your ideas and will be tempted to weed out the ones you see as being weaker and only show them the best that you have. You may want to turn your scribbles into a more finished visual and even put them into a deck to present them.

Don't.

Reviewing with a creative director should be a different experience to presenting work to a client. They are two contrasting meetings with very different needs.

A client needs a story that's more logical, going from problem to solution via some insights and possibly connecting to an agreed strategy. They're likely to want to see how the work will look and possibly how it will appear in the world. This is the polar opposite of what a creative director needs.

A creative director is used to dealing with the seed of an idea that's not yet fully formed and possibly just written down on a notepad, partly because this is how they work. They were once in the same position you are now – they're ideas people.

So, show them your ideas in their rawest forms.* They'll know which ones have potential and will help you to shape and grow them. You'll get much more from a creative review than going in with a couple of ideas you feel are ready to share with the client.

Creating ideas with larger groups can be effective. See **Beware of the brainstorm!** on page 135 to get some inspiration on how.

You don't need to put this in a deck. Focus on creating ideas at this stage, the presentation will follow.

IDEAS ABOUT CREATING IDEAS

MAKE IMPROVEMENTS
NOT
CHANGES

You will hear the word 'change' a lot in an agency or studio: 'Can we change this?' 'The client wants to change it.' 'Have you made those changes?'

Change can be positive as new media and technology forces us to adapt, grow and develop — and nobody can embrace change like a creative person. But change can often be negative, particularly when it could impact your work.

When this happens, we need to be careful. Making a change is fine, but those changes have to be improvements or what's the point in making them?

If you're having a discussion about changing the work, change the narrative and steer the conversation towards improvements: 'Can we improve this?' 'The client wants to improve it.' 'Have you made those improvements?'

This also something to be mindful of when, on reflection, you find a better way of doing something after it's been presented to the client. Nobody wants to say to the client: 'We've changed it.' They may have already signed it off and possibly got approval from their stakeholders too.

But let the client know you've improved the work... well, who could argue with that?

You may not agree with everyone's idea of an improvement. See *Pick your battles*, on page 139, to help guide you on when to push back.

PRE5ENT
HOWEV3R
M4NY
1DEAS
ARE
RI6HT
FOR
YOUR
PROBLEM

Most agencies will present a range of solutions to a client's problem. Usually — as with a lot of things — the magic number is three. Enough to show a range of thinking and offer a choice without there being an overwhelming number to choose from.

While this seems like an unwritten rule (maybe I've just turned it into a written one), the number of ideas you present doesn't have to be three.

I would advise against showing more. Providing too many ideas for clients to choose from shows your thinking doesn't have enough focus. It also shows there's no confidence — you're seemingly trying to throw ideas at the client in the hope they'll like something. You're also opening yourself up to the client choosing a blend of different ideas — the worst possible result following a creative presentation.

You can present fewer than three ideas if it fits the question you're being asked. If you have a tight brief (which is always the aim), then two ideas (is it A or B?) can be very powerful, particularly if those two ideas are totally different in their solution (and they should be).

If you have a very strong insight that leads to one inevitable and compelling solution, sometimes showing just one well-thought-out idea can work: 'We know that ..., so we believe the answer is ...'.

The choice of how many ideas to present to the client should be decided in the creative review phase by the team, but don't feel the need to always present three. Having the confidence to show fewer, more focused ideas can lead to a better, more effective result.

Read *The third idea you present should push the furthest*, page 149, if you do decide to go with the rule of three.

IDEAS ABOUT CREATING IDEAS

soul

Some work feeds your bank account, other work feeds your

Not many people know this, but as a creative you will have the opportunity to get paid twice for every project you work on.

The first payment is much like any employment, where you'll get money in exchange for your expertise. A figure that's agreed before the job and usually connected to a defined period of time.

The second payment comes in the form of something that nourishes your soul and fuels your creative fire. It makes you feel happiness through the process of creating the work and a great pride about the finished piece.

The double payment occurs when you're working on a great project that makes you happy and also pays well. Ideally, you'd like this to happen on every job, but that's not always possible. Make sure you are at least getting one payment or the other, and keep both your bank balance and your happy balance firmly in the black.

Notice when either of these is in the red, too. You may take a job that you're not thrilled about (not everything has the potential to be portfolio-worthy), but your bank balance needs a top-up. Equally, there may be a wonderful project where the pay isn't as good, but you'll gain something more valuable than a pile of coins.

It's likely that your dream brief will come from you. See *The perfect brief doesn't exist*, on page 93, to find out why.

IDEAS ABOUT CREATING IDEAS

NET-
WORK
beyond where you
WORK

Connecting with other people in the industry is key to your career. Your work can help build a reputation, but you also have to get out there, put faces to names and make connections with people.

This will either fill you with excitement or fear.

Remember, other creatives are always on the lookout for like-minded people they can collaborate with or recruit to join the agencies they work at. When creatives become creative directors and are responsible for building a team, you want to make sure it's you they think of when they're looking to hire.

For advice on finding like-minded creatives, see *Find your people*, on page 61.

Over your career, you'll make natural connections with people you collaborate well with. The more opportunities you give yourself to find those people, the more you'll give yourself the chance to land a job when your connections are looking for someone to be a part of their team (either putting your name forward for a position or contacting you directly). Make connections outside of your work bubble and you'll increase your chances of opportunities coming your way.

If you're the kind of person who thinks the idea of networking is hell, force yourself to speak to people. Even if that means you start by sending a brief direct message or joining conversations on social media. It's never been easier for the introverts among us to have a voice and be a part of it, so get yourself out there physically or digitally.

Beware
of the
brainstorm

At one point you would have been invited to a meeting along with most of the people in your agency. On entering the room you notice someone has raided the stationery cupboard and placed an array of pads and pens on the table along with some Haribo to keep the energy levels up. Once settled in, someone will stand up at the front, pop a slide on screen (or maybe go through a whole deck) and then ask if anyone has any ideas...

Hang on, this isn't a meeting. You, my friend, have just walked into a brainstorm.

There is value in gathering your greatest minds in the quest for a good idea, but the expectation that getting everyone together for an hour to crack the brief is a sure-fire way to not even make a dent in it.

If you want to foster greater creative collaboration and run some sessions with a wider team, make sure you:

- Use it as part of the process, not the process.
- Go in with a clear brief and plan.
- Give everyone the brief before, if you can, so people are prepared and even turn up with ideas.
- Give everyone a chance to share.
- Break down larger groups into smaller teams.
- Give people creative exercises to spark their thinking and focus their minds.
- Involve the same group at the end of the creative process too — help them see where the thinking went and what part the workshop (and their input) played in getting to the answer.
- Know when they're effective — bigger problems tend to require more focus and more time, with a small group of the most suitable experts.

See *Build your happy place*, page 73, for ideas on creating the perfect environment for creativity.

IDEAS ABOUT CREATING IDEAS

FAILURE
is your best teacher

On your quest for creative success, there will be times when things don't go to plan. In these moments you could feel like things have failed or that you or the work is a failure.

Try not to worry; there is no such thing as failing.

Every time something goes wrong, see it as a learning opportunity. Not everything is going to go right all the time and it's good to know and understand what happens when it doesn't. You will learn something from any kind of failure. And if you learnt something, you didn't fail.

Dust yourself off.

Take a deep breath.

Go again.

The more you fail, the more you learn. The more you learn, the better you are. And the more times you get up, the stronger you become. It's all part of gaining experience and you'll be all the better for it.

Treat any failure as a positive and you'll know what to do to improve. Take that learning into your next project, avoid the same pitfalls and it'll make your work even better.

Don't let failure get you down — see *Be kind to yourself*, on page 35, for tips on looking after your mental health.

IDEAS ABOUT CREATING IDEAS

PICK YOUR BATTLES

Your creative work and reputation is important. You will want every piece of work you create to be the best — in some cases, the best work you have ever done. So you will fight for your ideas when they come under threat. This is usually through feedback from either people within your agency or studio, or feedback from the client or their stakeholders. Their thoughts and opinions on the work may differ from yours, and you may feel their input is weakening the work.

Your instinct is to protect your work and fight them every step of the way. But if you take this approach every time you get feedback, you are likely to get a reputation as someone who is difficult to work with and doesn't work well with other people.

There will often be a compromise when creating work. Creativity is a collaborative process and can be the better for it, with different reactions and perspectives. You are creating work that aims to do a job and be effective, not art where everyone can form their own opinion and it doesn't matter.

So, take time to listen to others and take on board their thoughts and feedback. While they may not get across their thinking very well (and, in some cases, try to do the work for you), take a moment and try to see where they're coming from. Allow them to be a part of the work and the process. Your work, after all, needs to work for other people to be effective.

Concede on some things that may not be as you want but will still not negatively impact the idea. Always talk things through face-to-face and focus the conversation on the outcome the work needs to achieve and make decisions based on this.

See *Saying 'no' is no bad thing*, page 119, to learn more about the power of pushing back.

SMALL BRANDS

can provide your
biggest opportunities

We rarely have the opportunity to choose the clients we work with or the projects and pitches that come our way, but we all have brands that we admire and would like to create work for. Often, they can be big brands who are making brilliant work that you aspire to.

If a brand is already doing great work, you need to make sure you can not only match what's gone before, but hopefully improve on it. You may also find that big brands have more stakeholders and more hoops to jump through on the way to making more great work.

Smaller, lesser-known brands, however, tend to have fewer people, fewer hoops and therefore a greater chance to make something brilliant.

If they're a fairly new brand, they could be open to a lot of fresh ideas as they've not already exhausted every avenue. If they're a challenger brand, they could be braver in their approach, knowing they need to be disruptive to make an impact. They may also have a body of past work that's not to the level it should be, meaning you could help them make sizeable creative leaps through introducing them to better-crafted work.

Your thinking could also influence other parts of their business more easily too, like a brand idea that not only works in advertising but also transforms their packaging design. Or maybe, during your research, you have an idea that completely rethinks how they go to market — meaning your ideas can have a huge impact beyond advertising.

It's good to be inspired by the best work, but look out for the small brands when trying to make work that has an impact. They're the ones that often have the most creative freedom and the fewest barriers to making innovative ideas happen.

To make the most of every opportunity, you need to get yourself out there — see *Be your own Hype Man*, on page 85, for more.

IDEAS ABOUT CREATING IDEAS

BE THE SPARK

Energy. Enthusiasm. Positivity.

All these things are needed to create and make great work. So make these traits part of who you are and how you work. It will have an impact on the projects you work on and also those you work with.

Remember this every day you work. It's an easy one to forget when things are frustrating you or not going so well.

Great ideas happen when there are sparks.

Make sure you're one of them.

Learn about the positive power creativity has on people — see *Do more of what makes you giggle*, on page 29.

IDEAS ABOUT CREATING IDEAS

TO THINK OUTSIDE THE BOX,
make sure there's a box

Sometimes you will receive briefs and requests from people that use an array of terms to try and spark your thinking, letting you know they are looking for an idea that pushes the boundaries.

You hear phrases like: 'We want you to think big.' 'We're looking for something disruptive.' 'Let's think outside the box.'

This is rarely helpful as you are likely to always try to produce ideas that push the boundaries, ideas that have never been done before.

For commercial creativity to thrive, it doesn't need freedom or permission. It needs a problem, an issue, a constraint – a box.

So, the next time someone asks for thinking outside of the box, ask them for details about the box:

- Why does the brief exist?
- What's the barrier for the audience to do what we want them to do?
- What problem is the brand facing?

You're looking for the things that are constraining for the brand, the issues and things that are problematic. This is what great creative thinking needs. If you can clearly state the problem you're trying to solve, you'll have the perfect box to think outside of.

As well as defining the 'box', it pays to collaborate effectively with your clients. Read *The closer you are to clients, the closer you are to success*, on page 71, to find out more.

IDEAS ABOUT CREATING IDEAS

Leadership
is a mindset,
not a

Job Title

When we think about leadership, we often picture those who are leading the company: the chief executives, managing directors, head honchos, big cheeses, top dogs.

But being a leader isn't about a job title or even being part of the management team. It's a mindset, an approach, a way of conducting yourself and having an impact on others.

You may not think you have the ability to lead people or a company. Not everyone does. But ideas need leadership too and creative people have a lot of the right qualities.

If you stand up for good ideas, inspire and persuade others with their thinking, make tough decisions, are proactive and make things happen, act with integrity, work well under pressure, use your initiative and take responsibility — you're a leader.

You don't have to reach a certain level and you don't need permission to lead. While there aren't enough creative leaders in the boardroom, there are plenty in the creative department. So work on developing these skills as much as your craft and make sure you're leading.

—
Don't let a job title hold you back. See *You are not defined by your job title*, page 107, for more.

IDEAS ABOUT CREATING IDEAS

THE THIRD IDEA YOU PRESENT SHOULD PUSH THE

FURTHEST

If you are presenting three ideas (and no more) to a client, make sure your third idea pushes the client further. Even further than the other two, if you can.

You don't need to present that idea last, although it could provide a strong dramatic ending to your presentation. But include one idea that is more daring than the others.

Daring because it could require more money, use different media, not include the logo... There are many ways to push brands into new and unchartered territories.

Whatever it is, be brave. Don't always play it safe and never try to second-guess what your client might like. You never know how brave your client might be. At the very least, a more daring idea will provide a measure for what they see as pushing too far, giving you a barometer for the kinds of ideas, opportunities and territories where you can develop ground-breaking work for that brand.

Always look to include a wild-card idea on the bigger briefs to test your client's appetite for innovative thinking and they may just go with it.

See *Review rough thoughts, present finished ideas*, page 125, for more on developing and selling innovative thinking.

BIG IDEAS

don't always need big budgets

Creating a big idea is probably the most talked about deliverable for creatives. There are many definitions of what this is, but here's mine: a big idea is a single-minded thought that has the ability to be executed in various ways, across different types of media, and live in the hearts and minds of the audience for many years.

Sometimes you'll see a big idea for a campaign that kicks off with an epic TV spot. This could be followed by a series of smaller films across social media and digital out-of-home. These could feature a set of bespoke animations or each story could be shot by a different director. There may also be an elaborate stunt or brand experience or an app allowing you to play a game or shop directly from branded content.

—
Read more about big ideas coming from unexpected places — see *Small brands can provide your biggest opportunities*, on page 141.

While brands can throw a lot of money at executing a big idea, it doesn't always mean that the production will cost a lot of money. The term 'big' is about the size and value of the idea, not the size and value of the production budget. A healthy budget helps, but it isn't essential.

Obviously, the execution needs to fit the idea, so you should avoid trying to produce high-end executions on a shoestring, but there are ways to achieve this. Some brands choose user-generated content rather than big-name directors, while others rely on a series of simply crafted headlines rather than using any accompanying visuals. And a good approach is to always do fewer things better.

So if your project or client doesn't have the biggest budget, don't assume that big thinking isn't possible.

IDEAS ABOUT CREATING IDEAS

£?
KNOW
YOUR
WORTH

Ideas can launch businesses, sell millions of products, change people's behaviour, create culture, live in our minds for a lifetime and even save lives.

They can also generate a lot of money.

Budgets may be decreasing, but the impact of creativity isn't.

Pay attention to when the work you create gets results. When your ideas are effective and not only meet the objectives in your brief but even surpass them. Once the work has been released into the world, make sure you're asking if it worked.

See *Don't ever think you're the finished article*, on page 41, for advice on how to grow your potential value, not an ego.

Creatives are often poor at talking about money, preferring to avoid difficult conversations and bury their head in their work. But if you're consistently creating effective work, make sure you benefit from the success too.

If your work works, ask for a raise. If you're freelance, be clear on the cost of your services and what results you've achieved for other clients. If someone wants your expertise at a cut price, it's a sign they don't value you and it's best to walk away.

Perhaps there's a way to be creative with your pricing too – perhaps suggest a percentage of the profits from the success of the work rather than being paid for your time.

Creativity is valuable and brands and businesses can benefit greatly from your skills, so make sure you're getting what you deserve.

NO

day is wasted

There is nothing quite like the feeling of having an idea. A close second is the satisfaction of finishing an idea by making it. These moments nourish creatives and provide energy, as we feel like we're making good progress.

Some days, neither of those things or feelings happen. For whatever reason, we're just not feeling it. Ideas and any form of progress have stopped.

This is OK.

Your output some days may not be as prolific as others. But this doesn't mean you have achieved nothing. A creative mind needs time to do nothing. You need moments to absorb, reflect, drip feed things into your brain. And, of course, have time out and rest — even if this is during a work day when the expectation is work means being productive.

Sometimes producing nothing is productive; you'll just reap the rewards the following day.

See *Look after your mind: it's your greatest asset*, page 81, for more on the benefits of taking a break.

ENER&Y HARD WORK BEATS TALENT

Talent — the idea that some people are blessed with the ability to just create things — is often talked about when it comes to creativity. The truth is, we're all creative. Some of us lose our sense of childlike playfulness as we get older, while others put in a lot of hard work to improve our skills (skills that others simply see as talent).

There's one thing that beats any talent that you have: energy. Energy will power all of your hard work (the other attribute that beats talent) and fuel your enthusiasm for learning about your chosen craft and subjects you are working on. It will get you out of bed in the morning and fill you with the urge to start creating.

———
To find out how to bring your energy to a team, see *Don't wait for your ideas to happen*, on page 95.

Energy is also infectious. You only have to be in an agency when there's a pitch happening to feel it. When you have an energy about what you're working on, it can ignite something in others. This doesn't mean you have to be energetic in nature, leaping around and whooping at any opportunity. People with energy have an alertness, an excitement, an enthusiasm about what they do. You can see it in their eyes and feel it radiating from their very being.

As a creative director, energy is my number-one attribute when recruiting people. If someone has talent but no energy, they can be hard to work with and could even have a negative impact on the team. If someone has a slither of talent but bags of energy with a good work ethic, I can work with that, and the rest of the team will be energised by it too.

Make a note of what works*

*Heck, write a whole book.

This book is full of things I have picked up in my career. You will work with creative directors, peers and mentors who will teach you things too. There are also workshops, presentations, idea sessions, an agency's process and way of working, methodologies and more you can learn from.

Make a note of the things that work for you and also the things that don't.

One day you will be in a leadership position and people will look to you for the answers, for inspiration and for your direction.

Collect your experiences and use them to build and devise your way of working. Use it all to inspire your own leadership style and other people. These creative principles will be yours. They will be there to remind you of what's important and keep you on track — and also be something to share with and help other people.

Ideas and creativity is a gift. Pass it on.

You can only learn what works by doing. See *Done is better than perfect*, on page 45, for more.

Acknowledgements

This book exists because of the many people I have worked alongside who inspired and guided me along the bumpy road of creating and making ideas. Your advice is invaluable and something I carry with me every day. You may recognise some of the things you have told me here in this book, which you can take as proof that I was in fact listening.

Thank you to my wife, Emma. You are an inspiration. Particularly on claiming the title of being the first published Homent with your own book, 'Needlepoint: A Modern Stitch Directory' (available in all good book shops). I look forward to your second book, 'Next-level Needlepoint', where you will no doubt return the favour by plugging my first book and talking about how fabulous I am. My gift in return is your surname, which makes it very easy to find your books online.

Thank you to my mum and dad for supporting me throughout my career, which, let's face it, doesn't often feel like 'a proper job'. I guess you can tell people I'm an author now, if that sounds better/is more impressive/is much easier to explain.

Thank you to my sister, Nicola, who actually inherited all the artistic talent in my family, which has inspired me to work hard enough to be half as good. The hard work continues.

Thank you to Louis Loizou and Das Petrou for inviting me onto your podcast, *Orbiting the Creative Hairball*, to talk about my favourite subject: creativity. My notes in preparation were the beginnings of what turned out to be a whole book. It just goes to show what a simple brief can do for creativity.

Thanks to my editors, Beth Dymond and Emma Brown — you helped craft my words into what I really meant to say. Without your edits I would have repeated myself, rambled a lot and repeated myself. And thank you for pointing out when I'm being too self-deprecating. I'm such an idiot.

Thanks to you for buying this book. Unless of course I (or someone else) gave you a copy — in which case, go and buy one for someone who you think would benefit from the advice contained in these pages. Be the spark.

And finally (if it's not too meta), Martin, this book is for you. Not because you're now middle-aged and need all the helpful reminders you can get, but because you wrote the book you were looking for when you were first starting out and have needed during many moments throughout your career. It wasn't the book of short stories you planned to write this year, but remember, Done is better than perfect (*see page 45 for more*).

About the author

Martin Homent is a creative director from the UK who has worked both full-time and freelance within the creative industry for over 25 years, creating award-winning campaigns at global advertising agencies including Havas and TBWA.

Martin has built creative teams and businesses at a number of smaller boutique agencies and currently leads an in-house creative agency at one of the world's biggest brands.

He has also collaborated with his creative idol, Prince, on several projects including creating art for album covers, clothing and concert staging.

Outside of agency life, he pursues an art practice that includes printmaking and oil painting.

www.martinhoment.com
www.martinhoment.art

Printed in Great Britain
by Amazon